EARLY CHEVROLET
CORVETTES

Osprey AutoHistory

EARLY CHEVROLET CORVETTES

1953-67; all six-cylinder & V8s

THOMAS FALCONER

Published in 1985 by Osprey Publishing Limited
12–14 Long Acre, London WC2E 9LP
Member company of the George Philip Group

Sole distributors for the USA

Osceola, Wisconsin 54020, USA

British Library Cataloguing in Publication Data

Falconer, Thomas
    Chevrolet Corvette—the early cars 1953–1967:
    six-cylinder and V8 sports car.—(Osprey
    AutoHistory series)
    1. Corvette automobile—History
    I. Title
    629.2'222   TL215.C6
ISBN 0-85045-593-6

Editor Tim Parker
Photography by the author

Filmset by
Tameside Filmsetting Ltd, Ashton-under-Lyne, Lancashire
Printed by
BAS Printers Limited, Over Wallop, Hampshire

Contents

Chapter 1   *Route 66*   *8*

Chapter 2   **Sidescreens and V8s, 1953–55**   *14*

Chapter 3   **Winding windows and fuel injection, '56 & '57**   *31*

Chapter 4   **From four headlamps to four taillamps, 1958–62**   *47*

Chapter 5   **The Sting Ray, '63 & '64**   *80*

Chapter 6   **Disc brakes and Big Blocks, 1965–67**   *97*

Chapter 7   **To drive or restore, the Corvette hobby**   *116*

American model years and VINs   *126*

Specifications   *131*

Bibliography   *132*

Acknowledgements   *133*

Index   *134*

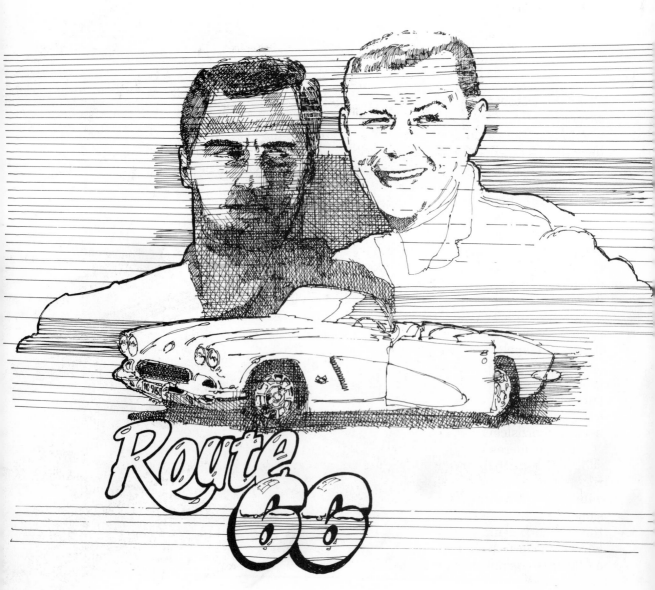

Route 66

Route 66

The date, October 1960; the place, the desert 45 miles east of Barstow, Arizona; the time, 11.55 in the morning.

A film crew is waiting for something to happen; they have that look of studied weariness which comes from a certain knowledge that seven days of filming gives only seven minutes of screen time and yet they are pioneers, for they are filming the first TV series ever filmed entirely on location. The location, the sunshine on Route 66, the legendary road that carves a great arc across mid-America, 2000 miles south west from Chicago through St. Louis and Missouri across the desert and down into Southern California, over the hills into Los Angeles.

Now the director hands his walky-talky radio back to his blonde assistant and shaded eyes go down to view-finders, a clapper board snaps shut as a beautiful white sports car sweeps into view over the top of the hill, its tyres squeeling gently on the hot black-top round the curve. Two clean cut, tanned young men can be seen sitting, quite high, behind the windscreen, wearing open-necked short-sleeved shirts.

As the cameras pan they are seen to notice a girl in shorts with wet hair and a wet tee-shirt waving from the roof of her '55 Chevy four-door which is sitting up to its windows in a shallow lake. Twenty-five years later those same boys might just drive on fearing an ambush, but this is the Eisenhower era and these young men are heroes, modern day Range Riders who drive endlessly along this romantic highway helping robbed widows,

Previous spread
In 1953 Joe Public thought a Chevrolet was a four-door sedan with duo-tone paint. Along came the Corvette. Look how low the 'Vette is? Note two girls in the sports car, Joe in the sedan. This is the original Motorama prototype

Left *Martin Milner and George Maharis, the stars of Columbia Pictures,* Route 66 *playing respectively Tod Stiles who owned the Corvette and his inseparable companion Buz Murdoch*

9

Top down in the desert, Martin Milner at the wheel, and George Maharis spot more trouble to fill another 50 minute black and white episode

lost teenagers, crashed pilots or injured pets. The actors are Martin Milner and George Maharis and they will make a total of 116 50-minute episodes of *Route 66*, inspiring a postwar generation to drive sports cars with tops down in the sunshine, not just in America but all over the world, for this is an enormously successful television series.

The car is the Chevrolet Corvette, a limited production, V8 powered, fibreglass two-seater and America's only true sports car. If the car hadn't been made, the series couldn't have been either. A pick-up truck might have sufficed but it could not have captured hearts and minds like this white two-seater Corvette.

The actors jump out of the car, slam the doors and go straight into the shade of the make-up tent, while the girl on the Chevy screams for her towel and a boat but the white Corvette just sits in the sunshine, its torturously routed dual exhaust system pinging and creaking as it cools, while the junior assistant mechanic uses a soft cloth to wipe the dust off the bumpers. It is a vehicle built for pleasure. Lower than any other car built in America, it has less accommodation and yet it shares a lot of the mechanical parts with their biggest selling sedan, the Chevrolet Bel Air, just like the one sitting in the lake.

The young mechanic opens the boot lid to pull out an oily rag, revealing a space only just large enough for two peoples' luggage, a rubber mat covering the spare wheel and this space artificially shortened by the motor and rams to operate the optional electric convertible top. He reaches over the driver's side door, the frameless window already lowered, releases the hood and pulls it up on its trailing edge to reveal an orange painted V8 with finned aluminium valve covers and a magnificent finned aluminium fuel injection system standing high between the cylinder banks. The young man checks the oil, water and brake fluid levels for the second time today. They never vary, even in this heat.

He feels an intense pride of ownership in this, his favourite of the two Corvettes used in the making of *Route 66*. What could be more delightful than to Simoniz those subtle curves or to burnish the doghouse of the Rochester fuel injection unit which breaths so much life into this willing little 283 cu. in. V8.

Right now he is not really thinking about the future but this young man will go on to own, and occasionally race, seven more Corvettes, three of them bought brand new, and in 25 years time will celebrate ten years of success with his own film production company with the purchase of a 1985 Corvette which will use a bored and stroked version of the same engine with this time electronic, not mechanical, fuel injection.

Twenty minutes later the electricians are at work on a second Corvette, identical to the first, which has been hooked up with an A-frame behind a flat-finned Chevrolet station wagon. Tiny flood lamps and a microphone have been mounted behind the top rail head of the windscreen with wires trailing back to below the tailgate of the station wagon which also houses the camera and the sound recording equipment.

Now Martin Milner takes the wheel, with the starlet in the passenger seat, while George Maharis perches on the rear deck.

The kid drives the station wagon and moves away, watching the activity behind him in his mirrors, the floodlamps shine on the actors' faces filling out the shadows caused by the high desert sun. As the camera rolls all three are reading from a hurridly retyped script held with drafting tape on the instrument panel and behind the grab rail on the Corvette.

Director Arthur Hiller orders the whole team back for lunch at the convoy of support vehicles and another seven minutes of Sterling Silliphant's script is in the can for another seven minutes of black and white television.

Up to now the kid has never been allowed to drive the

Tod and Buz leap over their 1960 Corvette in an early episode. The series was broadcast 8.30–9.30 pm every Friday night by CBS

Corvette but deliverance is at hand. No Corvette owner ever forgets the first time he drove one and what an opportunity is this. A stunt man has to be collected from the airfield in Barstow, all the other vehicles are in use and everyone else feels too tired with the heat, no one else wanting to drive the 45 miles without air-conditioning.

Everyone else is having lunch in the trailer as he leaves, fastens the standard equipment lap belt and checks his hair in the rear view mirror. The injected engine starts immediately. Leaving quietly he floors it in third once on the highway and the car is doing 90 before he shifts into top.

The hot road is empty, straight across the desert for ten miles, he slows to 80, a more comfortable speed with the top down and adjusts the sun visor, deflecting the wind nicely over his head. Relaxing his grip on the steering wheel the car runs true and straight, oil pressure at 60 lb, water at 180 degrees while the centrally placed tachometer shows 3700.

This is really it, he is a success. Not a 17 year old gofer from Long Beach on chauffeur duty to the airport but a Corvette driver. His left hand goes from the windscreen pillar back to the wheel while his right turns on the Wonder Bar radio. Two touches on the tuning bar bring up Johnny Horton and Hank Williams but the third is right on. Nelson Riddle's theme for *Route 66*. Checking that special smile he's been perfecting in the rear view mirror, he laughs just to himself and drives on down the hot, black strip of two lane highway towards Barstow.

Sidescreens and V8s, 1953–55

In January 1953 Chevrolet were making an extremely everyday and somewhat boring line-up of cars in the 150, the 210 and the Bel Air luxury range. Of the big three manufacturers Chrysler had the performance edge with their new hemi-headed Fire Power V8. Ford had a V8 as well, but theirs was the pre-war side valve or 'flat-head'. Chevrolet had not offered a V8 engine for more than 30 years although they had been building overhead valve engines for most of this time.

That month the Motorama, a travelling show case for General Motors cars opened at the Waldorf Hotel in New York and the centre piece dream car was a Chevrolet called the Corvette.

Previously there had been the Buick 'Y-job' of 1937, the Le Sabre of 1951 and the XP300 finished in 1952, but this Corvette looked as though it really could be built as an American sports car and sold at a Chevrolet price. As the Motorama show travelled the major cities the Corvette got a very enthusiastic reception and it was announced that the Corvette would soon be in production. By the end of June 1953 it was, each car being hand-built at a pilot plant in Flint, Michigan.

It takes more than six months to go from dream car to production and even Chevrolet was not really capable of such a feat. But the Corvette did go from being clay model to limited production car in 15 months which by any standards is an extraordinarily short time.

The driving force behind the sports car project was Harley Earl who had brought styling to mass production

Corvette books always start with a picture of the Motorama Show car, the EX122 prototype, so just to be different here is an early production car at the October 1953 Paris Motor Show. Licence plate says GM France and the car has been shod with Kleber Colombes tyres.

The detachable sidescreens are in position. This was the first public display of the Corvette in Europe. A weak franc, punitive duties and taxes and a patriotic home market means that there are still hardly any Corvettes in France

15

1953 interior had its instruments spread across the car, a matching cowl on the passenger side concealing the radio speaker. Centrally mounted tachometer had total revolution counter while the big red bulb just below the speedometer was the handbrake warning light. All '53s were two-speed automatics with a floor-mounted shift lever

for General Motors, and Chevrolet's new chief of engineering Ed Cole who would continue to champion the Corvette in his progress through corporate GM from head of Chevrolet, finally to president of General Motors itself. These two men had a special quality common to readers of this book but sadly very rare in the whole vast American motor industry, they were car enthusiasts!

The short gestation period was achieved in three ways. Firstly, the car was hastily though brilliantly conceived, with no time for development or changes of mind. Secondly, the production of the first 300 cars wasn't really production at all to a company like Chevrolet who produce cars by the million, and that

production didn't really start until 1954 when a line was established at St. Louis. Thirdly, and most importantly, the time and millions of dollars needed to tool up for steel body production was avoided by making the Chevrolet sports car out of fibreglass, as every production Corvette has been since.

In January 1954 production of Corvettes began on a proper assembly line, in a plant originally designed for building wooden bodies in the 1920s. The Corvette by the very nature of its fibreglass body would always be in limited production and was certainly not going to get an all-new plant, so the larger part of the St. Louis facility was always used for the assembly of other Chevrolet passenger cars and light trucks.

The 1953 door had two knobs; a larger front knob opened the door (there was no exterior release) while a smaller back knob released the side curtains. Below the armrest cover were big map pockets

One of three variations shown at the 1954 Motorama. This otherwise stock Corvette had front emblems in its hubcaps, external door pushes, winding windows and a hardtop virtually identical to that which would be introduced for the 1956 model

The Blue Flame Six used in all '53 and '54 Corvettes was pre-war in origin and could just be fitted under the low Corvette hood by use of coolant header tank running alongside the valve cover and three side draft carburettors with noisy bullet air cleaners. Quieter twin air cleaners replaced the bullet type in mid-1954

The car was unchanged except in minor details from the Flint produced car. The principal improvement was that the body panels were now produced in matched moulds for better quality fibreglass. The production line had the capacity to build tens of thousands of cars and yet only 4755 were actually made. Production was cut because even the Flint produced '53s were not selling as they should and the despatch area at St. Louis was filling up fast with stock piled '54s.

In retrospect it is easy to say that the car was funny and dumpy, perhaps underpowered for its size, and that the weather equipment, the leaky hood and detachable perspex sidescreens which were fine for the sports car set, just didn't go with the two-speed automatic transmission more appropriate for a luxury personal car.

1954 Corvette with top raised

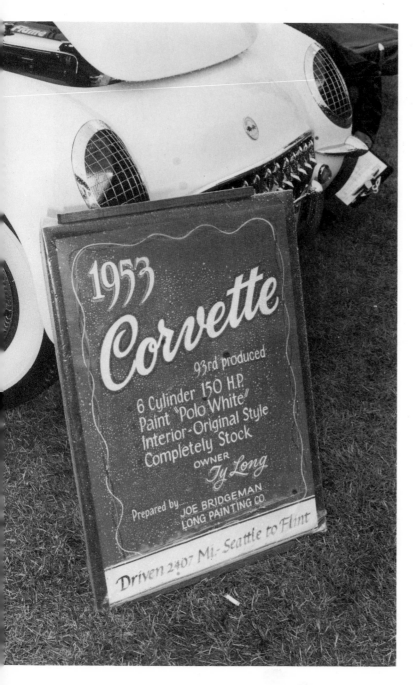

Far left *1954 with deck lid raised – this cover completely conceals the folded convertible top*

Left *Doing it right, driven to the show*

1954 Corvette – now very desirable. These were cheap ten years ago

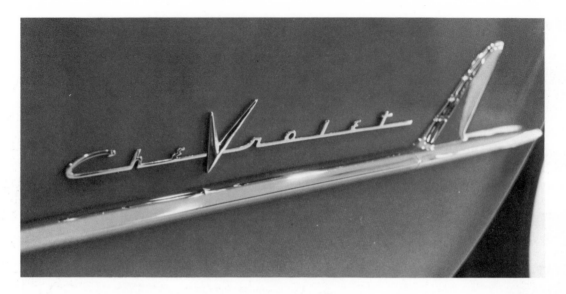

V8 '55s are distinguished by the big 'V' in the side script

The contemporary Jaguar XK120, which had been in production for many more years, sold to a defined market because it had just one four-speed transmission. But Jaguar offered in addition to their cutaway-door XK120 Roadster, a drop-head coupé with winding windows and a folding down, rather than detachable, convertible top.

The Corvette's top, of course, set a new standard for two-seater convertibles by folding, drop-head style, into its own well hidden compartment under a lifting body panel (like all Corvette convertibles to follow), but this did not compensate for the poor side screens.

Today six-cylinder Corvettes seem underpowered but at the time all the major imported rivals had four cylinders, except again for the Jaguar whose double overhead camshafts unit was only marginally more powerful if a lot smoother.

At the Motorama launch the car had an excellent reception from the press and public alike, everyone wanted one. Since they had only 300 to distribute throughout the 50 states and because the Chevrolet turned out to have a Cadillac price, the marketing men decreed that these six cars per state were to be

V8 was a better fit than the tall old six

*First Corvettes had a proper
trunk, sidescreens were stored
in bag vertically*

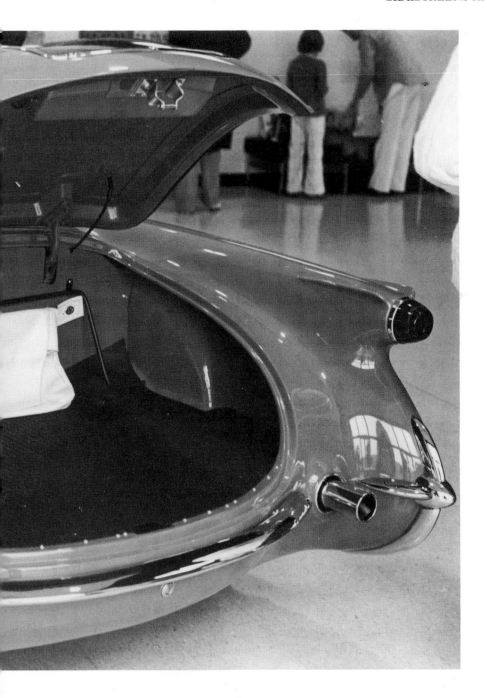

distributed to personalities and VIPs while other buyers were to be turned away.

The pent-up demand was not sustained by advertising and after that first summer was gone GM still did nothing about the weather-protection problems and the car started to get a bad reputation.

In 1955 a V8 was offered in the Corvette. The Blue Flame six was not a bad engine, it was just Chevrolet's only engine, but this new lightweight, overhead valve V8, that would become the legendary Small Block, made the Corvette fly. One of the most popular production engines of all time it would be fitted to half a million Corvettes.

Unfortunately in 1955 it still wasn't linked up to a manual transmission until very late in that year's production so the all important road-test cars were still automatics, and consequently the testers were luke-warm. So badly were the cars selling that in 1955 only 700 were built, only just over twice as many were hand-built at the Flint pilot plant during six months of 1953!

The Chevrolet navy had chosen a Corvette as their flag ship and it was about to sink with all hands! Of course the Corvette did not sink but instead got a new fibreglass hull and manual gears for 1956 but it is only recently, in the latter half of the 1970s, that these early cars have gained popularity and become collectable. Indeed anyone who had bought all the early Corvettes he was offered in 1970–75 could have seen a tremendous return on his capital. Today the '53s, particularly with low serial numbers, and '55s, are valued for their rarity, while '54s are still cheap enough to buy and use as 'drivers'. They have reliable and economical six-cylinder engines and all the virtues of rust-free fibreglass body-work which has always appealed to Corvette owners.

Now that even the cheapest cars have electric windows, putting your sidescreens into their special bag and strapping them in the trunk can become a ritual in itself, particularly as those components are now so rare and expensive.

CHAPTER THREE

Winding windows and fuel injection, '56 & '57

Sports cars are bought more for their appearance than their performance. The '55 Corvette, of which all but a handful used the new V8 engine, sold just 700 units. This was nothing short of pathetic, and simply confirms the sharp statement above.

To step out of a 1955, into a 1956 and race off down the road, you could be driving the same car. A drilled aluminium, three-spoked steering wheel replaced the two-spoker; the view down the hood was the same; the instrument panel was virtually unchanged while the brakes were, as before, barely adequate. The steering was good for an American car while the engine was as responsive as before. Only on stopping and getting out it would become obvious that the stylists had turned the Corvette from a car that was good for its time into one that was great for all time.

Their *tour de force* had been to carve a great scoop out of their clay model from the front wheel opening, way back into the door, and shave away the flares round each wheel opening. Headlamps were now standing up boldly, pointing the car in the right direction. At the rear, double-finned pods for the taillamps had been shaved away and these were now cut back into chromed housings. Instead of the full length, side chrome moulding which had visually split the car in two, it now looked all in one piece, strong, taut and raring to go.

By now the doors had winding side glass and external door handles and locks, and, as a curious throw back to the 1953 Motorama car, and helping the lines rather less either side of the windscreen, there were little fake air inlets. The number plate was now pulled out of its show car glass box in the trunk lid into a more conventional position in the rear bumper.

The stylists had achieved something very special because they had the freedom which was not available to them in the original Motorama car. Now the Corvette was specifically designed to be built of fibreglass and they were free to exploit the possibilities of this truly 'plastic' material in whatever way they wished. The Motorama car had been designed to be built out of steel, if necessary, and the rolled mouldings around the wheel

1957 interior with hardtop fitted. Basically similar to the 1953 it had three-spoke steering wheel. This RPO579E car has radio delete and column-mounted tachometer. The tachometer space in the dashboard was filled by a nose or rear deck emblem

openings of the '53 to '55 are characteristic of most mass-produced steel-bodied cars. The straight, clean-cut wheel openings of 1956 and later Corvettes right through 1967 were shared, of course, by the Jaguar XK120 already referred to, but then that started life as a show car too, yet with an aluminium body!

Under the bonnet the 1956 Corvette was launched initially with a 'dual quads'; twin, four-barrel Carters giving 225 brake horsepower with the 265 cu. in. V8, with a revised camshaft and an increase in the compression ratio to 9.25:1. Also now standard was the three-speed manual transmission which had found its

1957 chassis with fuel injection engine, four-speed transmission and heavy-duty brakes complete with air ducts. '53–'62 Corvette chassis are immensely strong but bumpers were not properly connected to chassis until 1958

1957 Corvette with narrow band whitewall tyres which were not available from the factory at the time. Only '56s and '57s have the air intakes at either side of the windscreen, aping the oil-cooler vent intake on the Cessna in the background. The '53 Motorama show car had these too

The 283 bhp, 283 cu. in. engine with cold air fed fuel injection. Since this was the only Corvette engine whose power output was rounded to the nearest 5 bhp it can be safely assumed that it probably gave rather more. But one horsepower per cubic inch made good advertising copy all the same

way into a few 1955 cars. *Road & Track*, the California-based magazine, picked up on this gearbox's ability to give a new Corvette 100 mph in second gear and they quickly followed with an enthusiastic road test comparing otherwise identically equipped Powerglide and three-speed models, the latter showing a top speed of 130 mph.

1956 also saw the first introduction of finned aluminium valve covers on high-performance engines. Supposedly a weight saving feature, each cover actually weighs one pound more than its stamped steel equivalent!

On the sand at Daytona Beach, Florida, a specially modified Corvette with just a flyscreen to protect the driver and a finned fairing behind his head achieved a two way, mean average speed of 150.583 mph. The driver was Zora Arkus Duntov, the brilliant Belgian-born engineer who had arrived at Chevrolet the previous year and who was destined to direct the future of the Corvette's engine, gearbox and chassis for a further 20 years. His first innovation had been the camshaft design which took his name and which gave the 240 bhp required to make this record run. The camshaft went into production the following year.

At the 12 hour Sebring marathon a Corvette managed a ninth place driven by John Fitch and Walt Hansgen. Chevrolet's advertising agency Campbell-Ewald dreamed up their famous advertisement 'The Real McCoy' with a shot of Fitch's Sebring car being refuelled in the pits at dusk. At last the Corvette was recognized as a potential success and even if barely 4000 were sold in 1956, it now looked like a great car, had a racing pedigree and was successfully changing Chevrolet's dull image—permanently.

By 1957 Ed Cole had been promoted to head of Chevrolet and he was determined that competition success would spur his division forward in the ceaseless battle to get more cars sold than Ford. In fact he did not actually get the sales that he wanted but that was of no

The 1957 Corvette RPO579E, one of approximately 20 made, with bonnet and boot open. American racing stripes were not part of this option

With hardtop on, and an everlasting fibreglass body Corvette owners need not fear the rain, though slippery roads demand special care on the original skinny cross-plies

'57 door panel, with winding windows

concern to Corvette enthusiasts. He wanted nothing less than fuel-injected engines available as options in every single Chevrolet passenger car model from the basic '150' four-door, right through to the Corvette. This would have enabled genuine production cars to outrun the opposition, not just in sports car races but in sedan/stock car races and in all classes at the likes of the Pikes Peak hillclimb too.

After early experiments by GM Engineering, a mechanical fuel injection system with individual nozzles located just upstream of each inlet valve was built by Rochester and with some careful tuning gave the Small Block, now bored to 283 cu. in., a fairly genuine 283 horsepower, a magic one horsepower per cubic inch. By 1957 Chevrolet had honestly built 2570 fuel-injected passengers cars, most of them two-door saloons, but 1040 were Corvettes.

The mechanical fuel injection was simple, robust and effective. It put Chevrolet right up there with Mercedes-Benz at the forefront of technology and did wonders for the image of the cars. On the road cars it was abundantly powerful, more frugal than a carburettor on an equivalent engine and looked marvellous under the bonnet. For track use, the engine would give full power when cornering while cars with four-barrel carburettors would cut out as fuel surged up the wall of the float chamber.

When a modern electronic fuel injection goes faulty or stops on the road, expensive parts and diagnostic systems and a tow truck to reach them are the usual solutions. The weak link of the Rochester mechanical system was always the drive cable from the distributor and a spare is easy to carry and fit. Mountain passes could also be a problem since unlike modern electronics, the system did not allow for variations in barometric pressure and the engine would start to run too rich.

While the three-speed transmission remained the base, a new Borg-Warner T10 four-speed was now available so that, at last, the Corvette had a full deck of cards and it is for this reason that the 1957 Corvette is considered to be such a classic.

To drive one today is a stirring experience. One wonders whether drivers then had a whole range of skills they do not have now, or if they just never used all that power under the bonnet. Even having got used to the big wheel close to the chest and the low geared steering with very little feel, the modern driver is amazed by the inadequacy of the skinny 6.70-15 cross-ply tyres. Even if the car had had better brakes, the tyres could hardly have coped and they also break traction in the lower three gears under acceleration, the live rear axle not helping at all. If the car is for daily use today then a change to non-original radials is essential and makes driving on wet roads a possibility as well. Sadly, the majority of 1957 injection Corvettes are now fully restored and little, if ever, used on the roads. Market forces have made them too valuable to drive.

The new convertible top was a smoother shape than the old, losing the hump of the '53 to '55 top and looked rather better when up because the new side windows were flat across their tops and not rounded like the old sidescreens. The power-operated folding top mechanism was introduced for 1956 as a $100 option. An electric pump at the back of trunk space powered hydraulic rams which lifted and closed the cover lid, and raised or lowered the hood frame. The rear bow still had to be dropped on to the closed cover manually. Chevrolet was so proud of their power-operated convertible top that it was standard on all early production '56 Corvettes, the

First year for the four-speed transmission was 1957

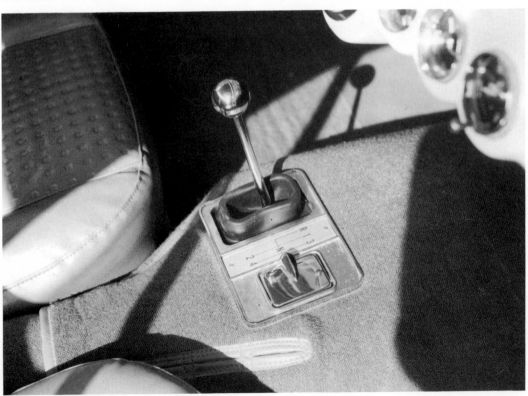

option of the manual top coming later in the year. The optional hardtop is one of the most beautiful made for any convertible. Strictly a two-man job to remove or replace, it is a light airy design with plenty of space behind the passenger and driver.

By 1957 only 20 per cent of Corvettes were being ordered with automatic transmission, proving that the Corvette was now becoming a sports and not a luxury car.

All Corvettes equipped with the Powerglide automatic transmission until early in the 1958 model year are especially confusing to anyone who has been driving for 20 years or less. 'Park' was the rearward position nearest to the driver followed by 'Neutral', 'Drive', 'Low', with 'Reverse' the most forward position. In 1958 the order

Tach drive distributor also drives fuel-injection pump

45

was changed to the modern style but reversed, LDNRP, with 'Low' at the front. The order was reversed again in 1962 to the familiar PRNDL. If someone offers you a spin in his pre-1961 Powerglide Corvette, take care! 'Reverse' makes a poor parking gear.

Even the most hardened enthusiast of the '53 to '62 Corvette will confirm that it is not a good handling car. That ten year period was one of almost unparalleled change with all the world's sports cars and the improvement to the Corvette, when it finally came for 1963, was long overdue. The new 1984 Corvette handles as well as exotics costing twice as much and has become the standard by which others may be judged. But the improvement of this car over the '63 to '82 cars was not so dramatic as was the '63 was to its predecessor.

The car had basic understeer problems, tending to plough on if a bend was taken at a constant speed. Power induced oversteer was quite possible and safe only in that it could be induced at ridiculously low speeds! Of course, driving sideways was the only way to go during the 1950s and to do it better Chevrolet made available their RPO684 bolt-on idler arm extension, starting in 1957, which changed the steering ratio to 16.3:1 from 21:1. Together with larger, stiffer shocks and springs front and rear and special cooling provisions for the brakes, this fixed steering ratio made control of the snaking rear end easier but at the expense of considerable parking speed effort. By comparison today, even Cadillac's ratios are less than 15:1.

The bolt-on idler arm extension is readily available as an after-market item and it is highly recommended. Once its limitations are accepted, the '53 to '62 Corvette is as much if not more fun to drive than most other cars of the era, and like any difficult car it is especially satisfying to drive well. On a dry, sunny day with the top down on an empty twisty country road you can hang the tail out 'till your heart's content and all within the speed limit. Front- and rear-engined Porsches may pass you as if on rails at indecent speeds but you will be having more fun.

From four headlamps to four taillamps, 1958–62

The 1950s was a decade of intense change in American automobile styling and Chevrolet made major changes to all its cars for 1958. The '55 to '57 Chevy passenger car range are now classics in their own right but there had been a general move towards longer, lower and wider cars with Ford and Chrysler getting theirs on to the market in 1957. With hindsight, a '58 Chevrolet sedan now looks awful but it was low and wide, with four headlamps, and the Corvette still boosting the Chevrolet image then got the same four headlamp treatment. The centre grille now had two less vertical teeth but new openings appeared on either side below the headlamps. The bonnet collected a washboard ribbing and the fake fender top air inlet scoops of the '57 were replaced by outlet vents in the cove area.

The trunk lid was given ribs while the taillamps were smoothed over with moulded plastic covers. To the purist who liked the previous year's cars, all these changes were for the worst but for the driver there were improvements galore. The bumpers were now big and tough, strong enough to leave the car parked on the street without worrying who might park behind. The exhausts exited still through the bumpers with eliptical openings. The front bumpers gave real strength to the car, were really well fixed back to the frame and gave first class protection to the dual headlamps which were a big improvement for night driving. Dash and instrumentation were completely revised and the random arrangement of gauges spreading towards the passenger

Beautifully lit studio shot of 1958 Corvette with hardtop. Narrow white tyres such as these were not available from the factory until 1962

1959 Corvette. This General Motors picture clearly shows the perforated hubcaps introduced that year to improve brake cooling

side was gone for ever. A tachometer mounted on the steering column had been a rare option on the '57s, and cars so fitted had the hole in the centre of the dashboard blanked with a big Corvette badge. Now everyone got the central tachometer, still with its total revolution counter, concentric with the speedometer and flanked by fuel, water, oil pressure and ammeter, all the instruments in a lovely moulded housing. This instrument package was set into a twin scalloped dash with a grab rail for the passenger who was in his turn faced with a shaped aluminium crescent reading 'Corvette' in extended lettering. Now the Corvette had an interior to go with its exterior, nothing on the car was aping the old imports from Europe; it was all truely American.

Cars with the optional wider wheels came with a smaller hubcap, and larger tyres

The '58 also got new door panels with separate armrests, S-shaped divider motif and twin safety reflectors for when the doors were open. Chevrolet agreed with popular opinion and removed the washboard and rear deck ribs for 1959 and made suspension improvements at the same time. These two extra features on the '58 do, however, make the model into a one of a kind car giving it a special appeal for collectors. The history of the Corvette has always been one of continual improvement and this author for one would rather have a '58 than a '57, the interior improvements and better instrumentation outweigh any misgivings about the external appearance.

The author's '59 discovered in an Inverness wood shed, Scotland. This car was registered in Lancashire in 1970 and then languished in Inverness for ten years with a frost damaged engine block. Complete with power top, hardtop and electric windows the car had been supplied new to GM in Antwerp

*Passengers grab rail and map
shelf*

Introduced with the 1953 cars, the tachometer included a six-digit total revolution counter which was one of those features which contribute to the cars eccentric personality; Porsche and Ferrari owners were quick to point out that they were standard equipment on farm tractors too! The total counter finished in 1959.

The high-performance engine for 1959 was still the fuel-injected RPO579D which gave a maximum 290 bhp with cold air trunking.

Suspension was improved with a new locating bar for the rear axle and improved again for 1960 with the addition of twin traction bars to prevent axle wind-up under hard acceleration but externally '60s are identical in appearance to '59s.

Ten years earlier in 1950, Briggs Cunningham had entered a standard Cadillac Coupe de Ville in the Le Mans 24 hours endurance race and the car had finished tenth. Now he entered a team of four near-standard cars, three injected 1960 Corvettes fitted with giant fuel tanks, Halibrand knock-off wheels and special oil coolers with considerable assistance from Chevrolet, while the fourth car was a prototype Jaguar E type, a fully disguised version of the Sting Ray's rival with still some months to go before its official announcement. In one of the wettest Le Mans ever, the John Fitch and Bob Grossman car finished eighth at an average speed of 97.92 mph; the pace woke up European enthusiasts to the Corvette's potential.

General Motors are great believers in styling continuity and Chuck Jordan now head of GM Design summed it up by saying 'We don't go from polished marble to jelly beans in one year.' While he was referring to the recent change of direction at Ford it has been a consistent policy even since the 1950s, established in the first instance when GM Styling, now GM Design, was GM Art and Colour. A radical new Corvette model, years in development, would not be ready until 1963 and it made a lot of sense to give the tail some new external panels and prepare the world two years early for the rear

Externally identical to the 1959, this is a 1960 fuel injection. Rated at 315 gross bhp, getting the power to the ground through their skinny 5.5 in. wide cross-ply tyres took real skill

1961 Corvette was the last year for the contrasting painted side cove and the first sight of the Sting Ray tail. Exhaust pipes discharged direct to ground behind the rear wheels

1962s have no stainless steel strip around the side cove, a new cove insert grille and a very practical anodized aluminium trim on the tuck under of the body. Engine was bored and stroked to 327 cu. in.

1958-62 Corvette's stylists really began to show their stuff during this period. The '58 'Vette was the first designed with dual headlights. In the cockpit, the horizontal gauge arrangement was replaced by a control panel which put all of the running instruments directly in front of the driver. And a center console was built in between driver and passenger. This feature, along with Corvette's original bucket seats and floor shift, started a trend that has made these items regulars on performance cars.

view which would be all other drivers would see of the new car as it sped past.

The 1961 update gave the car an altogether more feminine appearance, the nine grille teeth being replaced by a simple mesh; the headlamp bezels were painted instead of chromium plate and the old muscular boot flanked by a slightly separated curved rear fender was replaced by the 'duck-tail', the integrated look of the Sting Ray already in the offing. The trunk had slightly more capacity and its flat expanse was relieved by a longitudinal rib. Bumpers too were much less aggressive, simple quarter bumpers with no obtrusions and no holes for the exhausts to discharge through. Earlier bumpers had suffered a problem, particularly on the '58 to '60 cars, because the steamy and acidic exhaust gases released by non-emissioned engines running on automatic choke had caused serious rot problems. Now the exhaust was simply routed over the axle and discharged to ground immediately behind each back wheel. This also got over the problem of rattles and occasional fumes caused by the tortuous routing of the tail pipes on the earlier cars which ran through the body. Some owners of earlier cars adopted this simpler system but today, purists who drive their cars daily, opt for push-on pipe extensions to the standard system for daily use which throw the exhaust well clear of the back of the car, and remove those extensions for shows and rallies.

Forward visibility was improved for 1961 owners by the adoption of sun visors as standard equipment, they had been an $11.00 option since 1959. Windscreen washers became standard equipment in this year as well. Another improvement to the interior, which gave a little more space to the always very cramped cockpit of these cars, was the reduction of the width of the transmission tunnel by some 20 per cent.

As is usual procedure for Corvettes, the engine range went unchanged into the new shaped car. This was to be the last year of the 283 cu. in. engine after a five year run in the Corvette. The temperature control radiator fan

Left 1962 Corvette was the last Corvette to have a separate luggage compartment and the last American car to have a wraparound windscreen

63

White folks don't drive with the top down through downtown Detroit so much these days. Exhaust pipes went to ground out of sight behind rear wheels

A rare picture of a 1953 with its heater air-intake open. In the background at this GM launch at the Milford Proving Ground is one of the 1963 GS limited production racing coupes and Bill Mitchell's Sting Ray racer of 1959, first flowering of the String Ray shape

Left *1957. One of just 43 1957 Corvettes built with the RPO579E injection/performance package. Special wide wheels had small hubcaps*

Above left *'54s are mainly seen today at shows, hood and trunk open for inspection. '53 to '55 convertible tops and sidescreens detracted from car's appearance*

Above *1958 Corvette was brash with its four headlamps and fake mouldings, but interior was a great improvement over previous Corvettes*

Above *1963 injected coupe with optional aluminium wheels. This was the first Corvette which would carry a set of golf clubs!*

Above right *Factory fresh '65 injected coupe waiting for the dentist in Chapter Seven*

Right *1965 convertible, knock-off wheels, Small Block engine*

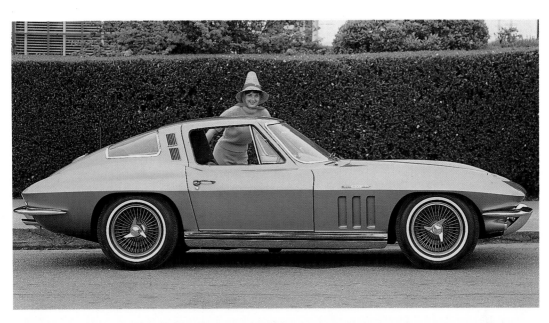

Right *The author with his 1966 convertible*

Below *1966 Big Block coupe with factory side pipes overlooking the Pacific in San Fransisco*

'67 Big Block convertible with side pipes, and factory headrests. The hardtop transforms the car for winter driving

Top *1967 coupe, restored by
its owner, waiting to be raced
against the clock at the
Goodwood circuit on a club
test day.*

Above *'67 Big Block coupe.
Hood stripes were factory
applied and colour
co-ordinated with interior*

using a silicon clutch which free-wheeled until the engine was too hot, an option the previous year, now became standard, releasing more horsepower for use at the rear wheels. In spite of the introduction of an aluminium case for the four-speed transmission which was the most popular option and gave a 15 lb weight reduction and the removal of all that front and rear chrome, the '61 still weighed 50 lb more than its predecessor.

For 1962 the stylists omitted the chrome strip round the side body cove and a fine tooth grille replaced the three ribs in the cove vent. To compensate for what might have been a heavier appearance of the plainer side cove, a new ribbed rocker panel now covered the tuckunder of the body and sharpened-up the often stone damaged and rather wavy appearance of this area when it was painted. At the front, the aluminium grille was changed in detail and finished in black.

The more elegant appearance of the 1962 belied its performance, for the bored and stroked engine now gave an extra 20 horsepower on the base unit at 250, and an extra 45 horsepower on the optional fuel-injected engine. The 'dual quad' twin four-barrel arrangement, optional since 1956, was now abandoned in favour of a single Carter AFB carburettor on the high-performance, non fuel-injected engine option. The 'dual quads' were never easy to tune and could be hard to drive in the mid rpm ranges.

Except on fuel-injected Corvettes, the tachometer drive had always been from the back of the generator. With the introduction of the 327 engine for 1962 this rather curious and untidy arrangement was abandoned in favour of drive via a worm gear from the distributor, as on the injected cars. These worm gears were not usually good for the life of the car and continued to be an expensive item to replace on all Corvettes until tachometers went electronic in 1975.

For the driver at the wheel there was more power at the pedal but otherwise changes were minor. The heater

1962 with hardtop

Rear view of the '62 shown on previous page. Note the heavy licence plate surround which doubled as a bumper

Above left *1962 rear emblem*
Left *1962 front emblem*

was now standard rather than the $102.25 option although this was deleted on export cars, export being a euphemism for Hawaii, where it really can get cold sometimes but no one is allowed to admit it.

As every year since 1956 the hardtop was available as an alternative to the folding soft-top, or both could be ordered for an additional, in 1962, $236.75.

On cars with the hardtop only, additional luggage space was available on top of the fuel tank in the soft-top stowage area and this could be accessed by releasing the front hardtop clips and the rear deck button. Enthusiasts at the time would devise props to hold them open, like fighter aircraft canopies awaiting the call to 'scramble!'; Corvettes are rich in symbolism.

1962 door interior

A 24-gallon fibreglass fuel tank became a regular rather than limited production option for 1962 and used the convertible top stowage space, making it available only for the hardtop cars. The tank was strictly intended for racing. With petrol at just a few cents a gallon one did not need to accumulate it where it was cheap and it would be a hardy soul who endured driving the car 500 miles non-stop to take advantage of the range this tank would give.

Automatic transmission '62s had the conventional PRNDL to bring them into line with modern automatics and the transmission case was changed from iron to aluminium. A neutral safety switch had been introduced the previous year.

Fresh air intake on 1962. Air-conditioning was not available until the new 1963 model

The Sting Ray, '63 & '64

After ten years of production during which a total of 90,000 rigid rear axle cars were built, an entirely new chassis was introduced with a choice of two new bodies, a convertible or fastback coupe.

The 1962 engine line-up was carried through unchanged for 1963, together with the choice of three- or four-speed manual gearboxes or the two-speed Powerglide automatic. Everything else about the 1963 Corvette was absolutely brand new and in the showroom it was an immediate sensation. Clues about the styling had already been given in the Sting Ray racing car, first seen at Marlboro MD Raceway in April 1959, but now that shape had been subtly honed by waisting the body at the doors, thereby emphasizing the wheels. The split bumper look was retained at the front and at the rear, the tail resembling that on the '61 to '62 cars but having no components in common. There was no luggage lid, the luggage compartment now being a space behind the seats and shared with the stowed top in convertibles.

The '53 to '62s had had their fuel tanks within the wheel plan but now the fuel tank was at the very rear of the car above the rear frame wheels and filled with a racing style, 4 in. diameter centrally-mounted orifice and an even larger diameter hinged cover with a traditional Corvette crossed flags emblem. Although the wheelbase of the car had been reduced by 6 in. from 102 down to 96, the extra space now designed into the passenger compartment gave the driver much greater comfort and a feeling of being at one with his car, something entirely

Right Widely published, these GM publicity pictures of the '63 convertible portray a pre-production mock-up; note the fabricated windscreen trim and other body details. If this was a road-going car the optional knock-off wheels should have fallen off within a few miles – right-hand side spinners have been fitted to the left side of the car!

1963 Corvette had a roomier cockpit and better driving position. Distributed by Chevrolet public relations as a typical stock '63 interior, this is actually a pre-production mock-up. Note the full sweep minor instruments, lettering to instrument faces and the trip odometer set into the time clock face

1963 327–340 horsepower with headlights raised. Briefly owned by the author, this car runs 70-profile radial-ply tyres, giving delightful handling in the wettest conditions. Radials were not factory fitted by GM until 1973

This page and overleaf *This superb brace of '64s belonged to a Florida enthusiast and his wife. She gets the air-conditioned coupe while he drives the aluminium-wheeled convertible*

missing from the previous generation of Corvettes. The front glass was steeply raked, giving it a squarer proportion and the chance at last to use decent sized windscreen wipers while for the first time the Corvette did not have the traditional 1950s wraparound windscreen but steeply raked door pillars with crank operated window venti-panes. These were to prove to be the most popular means of entry for car thieves until they were abandoned in 1968.

The new chassis gave the Corvette an up-to-date front suspension with the uprights supported by upper and lower ball joints rather than the king pins used previously. This in turn allowed the introduction of an assisted linkage power steering with a conventional engine-driven hydraulic pump straight out of the GM standard parts bin. Although the '63 was running skinny 6.70 × 15 cross-plies the chassis was destined to handle progressively wider tyres and then big foot printed radials from 1973 onwards. As we shall see, new engine options brought with them greater weight and the trend to power steering, though not always ordered, made these engines really practical for daily use on the street.

The power steering system featured a separate telescopic ram and control valve on the end of the Pitman arm and is remarkably generous in the amount of feel that it left in the steering. Like so many other

Left and above 1964 publicity shots. One piece back window on the coupe, new lower side trims and lack of metal inserts in hood identify 1964 models

items on this remarkable design it was to remain virtually unchanged for a 20-year production run.

Compared with the powerful sports cars of the time, Ferrari, Aston Martin, Maserati, Porsche, Lotus and Jaguar only the last three had independent rear suspension and the German car, being rear-engined had to be independent almost by definition. The transverse underhung rear road spring cleverly kept the weight down low and the whole rear suspension system neatly underneath the chassis, allowing a flat rear luggage compartment and avoiding any spring mountings on the chassis itself. Like the Jaguar's system it used the double-jointed drive shaft as one member of the parallelogram. Problems with the system are confined to

Rear deck lid hides the convertible top, which can be lowered and folded away by the driver alone without leaving his seat

occasional breakage of the bottom leaf rear spring, which brings the spring into sharp contact with the road, a fair appetite for universal joints for the drive shafts and collapse of the spindle bearings due to inadequate maintenance or the fitting of excessively wide wheels. Drive shafts have to be disconnected from the spindle to permit greasing: with the correct greasing tool this is an easy job.

The reduction in unsprung weight, and the end of the axle tramp of the old live axle car were great advantages but the improvement as felt from the driving wheel makes comparison with the earlier cars superfluous.

Introduction of the coupe body style was a big surprise at the time but it was a logical step. A fibreglass sports

This 1964 327–300 has the air-conditioning, never available on the previous series of cars, which opened up new markets for the Corvette, particularly in the rapidly expanding cities of the sunbelt

body with full-size doors but a conventional steel chassis can never be as stiff as a car with a full roof, offering lots of rattles and squeaks. For an illustration of just how much the body moves, try jacking any '63 to '67 convertible at the recommended rear jacking point and watch the rear door gap open!

The racers were quick to see the advantages of the far stiffer coupe structure, but the stylists had also given it a special and separate appeal which broadened the market for the car. The fastback tail and the divided back window emphasized the pointed junction of all those curves and gave the car the kind of visual interest and dynamic feel that were attracting General Motors' styling a new kind of respect from fellow professionals around the world. It was an affordable dream car.

Air-conditioned 1964 with original rear window sticker

The rear window of the coupe drew heavily on military aircraft symbolism, the doors were cut up into the roof as though it were a fuselage, and made it easier to get into the car.

When the hardtop was ordered in the open version of the car, it gave it a fresh and different appearance emphasizing the taught 'belt' line of the car while the convertible top emphasized the torpedo shapes of the rear wheel housings.

Concealed headlamps, rotated by electric motors were a postwar American first and kept the headlamps clean until they were required. They take a few seconds to rotate into position and presumably because of resistance in the longer cable, the right-hand one is always slower to lift than the left.

Ground-up restoration – 1963 fuel-injected four-speed chassis waiting for the body to be dropped on. One of the most successful sports car chassis of all time, it was eventually used for more than half a million Corvettes through 1982

The new body now had space to incorporate factory air-conditioning, and customers from the southern States were quick to appreciate the combination of this and the small volume interior that gave a car that was cool in more ways than one.

Leather seats were available in 1963 for the first time but only in one colour, saddle; other interior colours being supplied in vinyl. There were few mechanical changes for 1964, principally the uprating of the L76 engine by 25 horsepower with the use for the first time of a Holley carburettor and an extra 15 horsepower for the fuel injection.

A thicker and stronger gearshift lever with a heavy chromed knob and a much improved action indicated that the four-speed car was now being delivered with the new Muncie M20 or M21 close ratio gearbox instead of the previous Warner T10.

On the coupe the divided rear window was removed, too many drivers having found that, combined with the centrally placed interior mirror, it gave a blind spot that neatly hid a police motorcycle!

The 1964 seats were available in a wider range of colours in leather, had an improved design of backrest and the rake adjustment of the lower squab was discontinued, the underseat storage compartments having been discontinued in mid-1963. The driver's instruments still had their needles coming out of deep recesses but these were now the same black as the instrument faces. Externally the hub caps and fuel filler emblem were new and the bonnet lost its trim panels but retained the indentations.

Coupe production for 1963 had been virtually half of the total but by 1964 it had dropped back to a third and remained in this proportion for the duration of this body shape. Yet only 11 years later convertibles were phased out permanently in favour of Targa roofed coupes due to lack of demand. Such is the nature of public demand and the Corvette's continuing success was the proof of its response.

Disc brakes and Big Blocks, 1965–67

Seen at a distance of 20 years, the Sting Ray Corvette was the first of the great ones. Its handling was so good that it flattered the driver, going where it was pointed by the steering wheel and feeding back just the right amount of information through the seat, the wheel rim, the pedals and the exhaust note; a classic 1960s sports car. No need to fight it through the bends or anticipate a sudden break in traction over an unexpected bump; it could be driven safely and predictably, even with the tail broken away, the slide controlled on the throttle and the big three-spoke wheel.

It was the coming together of two eras. The high compression unrestricted V8 engine of the late 1950s, which needed heavily-leaded high-octane petrol – this fuel disappeared from road side pumps in the very early 1970s, but is still used by private aircraft – and the era of today's underpowered but good-handling cars which truly started with the introduction of independent suspension in mass-produced cars at the beginning of the 1960s. Developments in radial-ply and much wider tyres mean that most people today drive cars whose handling is far more capable and far exceeds the performance of the engine. Modern sports cars have so much grip in the wet or dry that to drive on the limits of traction and to enjoy the pleasures of broadslides on country roads is only for the very brave or very foolish.

The '63–'64 Corvette failed in one important area and this was its brakes. When drum brakes got hot the drums expanded away from the shoes and the pedal softened.

They were good for just one high-speed stop, and could pull unpredictably at any time. The J56 sintered-metallic brake package improved the situation but they needed to be warm to work properly and were even more unpredictable in daily street use than the normal production brakes.

1965 was the year that disc brakes were introduced, the year when Corvette owners and enthusiasts could look squarely at any other sports car and not feel embarrassed. They knew too that while the Corvette may have been more cheaply executed it was certainly more durable because of its indestructible fibreglass body.

Owners of '63 and '64 Sting Rays see two advantages of their drum brakes. They give better fuel economy, because unlike the disc brake they lack the constant rubbing friction of the spring loaded disc pads, and do not suffer from any of the corrosion problems which are described later.

If 1965 was the first year for brakes that could at last match the Corvette's performance, then it was also the last year for fuel injection which had been such a successful production option since 1957. It was ousted by the Big Block Mark IV engine which could give more solid performance for half the cost.

The Corvette buyer in 1965 was spoiled for choice with five 327 engines ranging from 250 hp up to the 375 hp fuel injection and the 396 cu. in. Big Block which came with a single Holley carburettor, a hood bulge with chrome side louvres and heavy-duty front and rear suspension with a rear anti-roll bar.

Only 771 fuel-injected engines were sold compared with nearly twice this number in 1964 alone, while the 396 sold 2157 in its first year. By 1967 more than half of all the Corvettes sold were ordered with Big Block engines.

Capable of giving 14-second standing quarters and 0–60 times of less than six seconds straight out of the showroom, these were fabulously powerful engines but

Left Hub caps are different for every year '63–'67. This 1965 has the new functional side vents and the lower trim panel exclusive to that year. Over 120 mph, the aerofoil section front body causes front end lift problems

Right 1965 optional aluminium knock-on wheel complete with correct original Firestone Super Sport tyre. Note the correctly fitted spinner on the left-hand side of this car. The spare was also aluminium and the tool kit contained a mallet

Left *All original 1965 327/350 with factory air-conditioning. Stainless steel shielding around distributor prevents radio interference. The air cleaner has been removed to show the single Holley carburettor and cast-aluminium inlet manifold*

Above *1965 four-speed convertible with electric windows and telescopic steering wheel. Ticket on radio tuning knob gives instructions for radio tuning*

had more than their fair share of disadvantages when fitted to the Corvette. Weighing some 680 lb they changed the balance of the Corvette into a nose-heavy car and the difference is obvious to the driver. They extract a 25 per cent penalty in fuel consumption compared to the Small Block engine but worst of all they are nothing like so reliable. Even the most careful buyers cannot know what previous owners have done to their Big Block engines and it only seems to take a brief period of over revving or mistreatment of the cold engine to make the oil pressure gauge dive to the left and to make the crankcase sound like a busy shipyard. And when the time comes to rebuild, only the best components and the most careful assembly will avoid a repetition.

1964–71 was the Big Block era, the first of the 'muscle cars' being the Pontiac division's GTO which had the 389 cu. in. engine out of the big Grand Prix put into the lightweight two-door Tempest intermediate body. It made a raw and exciting, but underbraked and ill-handling combination which became a legend within months. The muscle car era began with its massive

Far right A powerful heater, rearward weight bias, and a limited slip differential make a Small Block Corvette a marvellous snow car

Below right Thick with road salt, the author's black 1966 photographed en route to collect a hardtop and five original aluminium knock-offs

Below Four-pot cast-iron brake calipers introduced in 1965 were immensely powerful, prone to corrosion problems if brake fluid was not changed annually. All four discs are ventilated. Note the bolted-on adaptor with locating pegs for the aluminium wheel

associated advertising and started every American car maker trying to copy the GTO and turned every male American under the age of 50 into a high-performance expert. At this time, every American town had a dragstrip as well as illegal street races on the outside of town and standing quarter miles were the benchmark by which cars were compared. The Corvette, which did everything else so much better than any of them, did not always measure up well against these live-axled lightweights. On a real live road with a few bumps in it, the Corvette with its independent suspension could out-drag them all.

To go with this vast choice of engines, the Sting Ray was still available as a coupe, convertible or detachable hardtop, manual or automatic; air-conditioning and power assistance meant that you could specify any stage from gentle personal car for shopping, to a fire-breathing racer.

Along with disc brakes came a number of appearance improvements. There were no indentations in the hood, and the air outlets behind the front wheels became a functional three-louvre grille borrowed directly from the Ferrari 250GTO road racing car, a mark of respect perhaps for the car so beloved of the styling staff.

In keeping with the functional theme the dished instrument faces were made flat and a one-piece moulded door panel, a vinyl/foam/cardboard composite sandwich unduly prone to cracking was fitted and every Corvette would get these for the next 12 years. On the previous years car the screwed-on plastic armrest had also pulled the door shut but now, a soft plastic door pull was added towards the front of the door. This was replaced for the last two years of 'mid-year' production by a much superior metal pull handle, which was more in keeping with the car's sturdy character. Seat pleats became lateral rather than longitudinal and the convertible's top lid had a plain rather than ribbed trim strip. Also new for 1965 were, inevitably, a new design of triple-eared hub cap trim for the standard steel wheels, a new fuel

As in previous years the factory hardtop was available as an alernative or optional extra to the soft-top. Fitted, it subtly changes the shape of the car. Rear window is plexiglass, bonnet and side emblems on this 1966 show that it is a Big Block

filler cap lid emblem and an air intake grille with black centre bars.

The author has a particular affection for 1966 Corvettes having bought a manual 327/350 convertible in 1971 while a student and having sold it (in favour of a 1974 convertible) eight years later. During this time it went from being economical student transport to a tax-deductable business car, did vacation trips through Holland, Belgium and France, was drag-raced, and hillclimbed. Apart from a prodigious appetite for rear universal joints, two clutches in 50,000 miles, one set of replacement rear wheel bearings and 80 Champion J6 spark plugs it was entirely trouble free, and averaged 18–20 Imp mpg over the eight year period of ownership.

Purchased with five-slot 7 in. aluminium wheels which drowned the front brakes in heavy rain, the author was able to swop these for a set of five factory knock-offs from a man in Birmingham who thought they were too narrow! In fact the aluminium wheels at six inches are half an inch wider than the standard wheel.

Like most Corvette owners the author bought his car used. Choosing models, options and alternative power trains is the privilege of new car buyers, the rest of us have to take what we can find and the majority of Corvette owners buy what happens to be local to them when they are in a buying mood.

The author happened to spot his car on a garage forecourt, the owner was keen to sell it and asked for £1100 because he could not get the brake calipers to seal properly. The author might have preferred a 1967 with its properly positioned parking brake lever instead of the inconvenient underdash device but then the car would have been wrong with those wonderful triple-eared knock-off wheels.

Detailed examination of the brake calipers showed that all 16 bores had been badly pitted by rust. The car had been stored in a damp garage for four years before it was bought. The brake fluid, being hygroscopic, had absorbed water from the atmosphere and the rusting had continued while the car sat. The bores were reamed lightly, the seals replaced on them, but for a period the brakes had to be bled every few hundred miles.

In the end a set of second design calipers and pistons were imported, at staggering expense, the second design type first being used in 1967. The first design fitted originally to all 1965 and 1966 cars had a hard, round, plastic insulator on the pad end of each piston to insulate the brake fluid from the heat of the brake pads. Presumably the enthusiastic pre-production testing had shown this insulator to be necessary to avoid boiling the fluid but most road drivers never have this problem. Since the pistons are made of aluminium, salty road spray penetrates between the insulator and the piston and the resulting corrosion expands, breaking the piston and allowing it to come too far out of the bore.

The modifications to the piston were the only improvement that GM ever made in 18 years of production of these brakes, their view being, no doubt, that if brake fluid was changed annually then the corrosion would never take place. Most Corvettes over five years old have been fitted with exchange calipers bored and sleeved with stainless steel and a number of after-market manufacturers now produce these.

The old 1966 was a most satisfying car. With its optional close ratio Muncie gearbox and 3.70:1 axle ratio it beat all comers at the local dragstrip. Letting the clutch out sharply at 3500 rpm and breaking traction on the line worked best with the narrow tyres, the same technique with wide tyres or slicks would twist rear spindles or break the differential inner housing. The author eventually fitted a 3.36:1 axle which made long drives rather more peaceful and 20 mpg practical at 75–85 mph.

Not a lot went wrong, the oddometer gave up at 51,000 miles, a replacement gear was easy to fix. Few of these gears last longer than this, indicating that mileages are rarely truthful. The tachometer horizontal drive gear in the distributor failed and was replaced. The

1966 Big Block. First year of the 427, the bonnet was the same as 1965 and incorporated functional air vents

plated diecast front parking lamps corroded through from the back, another common problem on this year but like most other parts on the car, they are still available. The tail pipe trims in the rear rocker panel suffered the same fate, the stainless ones fitted in 1963–65 were a much better design.

The 1966 differed in other ways from the 1965, it had a vertical rather than italic Corvette script front and rear, a fluted rocker panel trim, a diecast honeycomb grille, once again new hub caps for the steel wheels and a new fuel filler emblem. The 1966 seats also had more of the lateral pleats. The fuel-injected engine was gone, so were solid lifters for the Small Blocks, the Holley carburetted 327/350 being the most powerful. The Mark IV was enlarged to 427 cu. in., a full 7-litres and offered the choice of mild 390 hp or wild 425 hp.

A magnificent pair of outside exhausts became available in 1965 for the Big Block engine and the more powerful Small Blocks which used the 2.5 in. exhaust. In 1966 and 1967 they were available for all ranges. They were not a tubular header design but connected straight to the original cast-iron manifolds. To prevent the drivers and passengers legs from getting burnt too badly they had a perforated metal heat shield over the chambered side pipe. 1963–67 exhausts are noisy and not recommended for long journeys. When they were fitted at the factory a special lower rear closing panel was used without exhaust pipe holes. Rear luggage racks became available in 1965 as well, they were dealer-fitted to both coupes and convertibles when required.

The appearance of the interior of the '65 to '67 car was much improved by the use for the first time of press-moulded carpet which makes a much neater installation. Unfortunately, it is also a lot more expensive to replace.

Many owners of '63 to '67 cars never discover the remarkable range of adjustments made available for them by the factory. The steering track arms have two positions for the track rods giving fast and slow steering positions, power-steering cars being already set in the fast position, the rest delivered in the slow rearward position. Moving to the forward position and resetting the tracking is an essential move. Even non-telescopic wheel cars have some inches of column adjustment available (see the manual for details). On the transmission side the throw of the four-speed shifter can be adjusted for long or short, though the gearbox and linkage need to be in first class order to enjoy the short throw position and the clutch pedal has an ingenious adjustment for long or short travel, the latter position requiring a strong left leg and is perhaps best left for the racetrack.

The worst mistake the author made with his '66 was

1967 with the new wider Rally wheels, five-louvre air vent and no side emblems, the cleanest model of them all

1967 L88 – sheer brute horsepower

to fit a set of tubular exhaust headers 'for increased horsepower with significant improvements in fuel economy'. They did neither, sounded terrible, hit the ground over bumps and rusted through in less than a year. Fortunately the original manifolds were retained and the effect of restoring them to the car was to bring back all the old smoothness, fast warm-up and back to 20 mpg again. Ten years later, headers have not improved and those who fit them for the most part seem to be just as disappointed.

1963 is the classic year for the split window coupe but not so much the convertible. 1965 is the classic year for the last fuel injection but not so much the other engines, yet 1967 is the year when they were all classics, the fifth year of production when they seemed to get just everything right. At the rear you got four taillamps as well as a reversing light.

Inside, the handbrake was at last positioned between the seats though it still lacked the power to do handbrake turns! For the Small Block, the bonnet was now devoid of ornamentation and there were new five-slot side vents, this time in the style of Maranello's 275GTB.

1967 hardtops came with an optional black vinyl finish, and the coupe headliner was moulded around the sun visors. The seat backs had side release levers so that they positively locked back, in common with all GM cars starting that year, while the passenger no longer had a grab handle hole moulded into the glovebox upper cowlings. The rear edges of both doors carried reflective 'GM mark of excellence' badges.

Externally, road wheel widths were increased by half an inch to six inches and for the first time a two-piece wheel trim was used, shared by the Division's Camaro Z28 models. Since the Government had now outlawed the aggressive eared spinners on new cars, the aluminium wheels were redesigned to be fixed direct to the hub with five nuts with an ornate matching centre cap to cover these. This meant a significant reduction in unsprung weight because each spinner and adaptor assembly which was now omitted weighed a full 4 lb. These were the last Corvette aluminium wheels for nine years and the $263.30 that they cost bought you the spare one as well. Not until 1976 were aluminium wheels offered again and then you only got four of them.

1967 was the peak year of the Big Block sales. Never before and never again would it happen that more than half the total year's production would use this engine. For 1967 a special hood was introduced with the facility to collect high-pressure cool air from the base of the windscreen. Only 20 of the 22,000 cars built this year actually used this cold air facility and they were the L88s. Rated at only 430 bhp in the sales literature they cost a suspicious $947.90 and could only be ordered with the heavy-duty brake and suspension package, no choke, no heater and no radio to discourage those wealthy buyers who liked to check all the boxes on the order form. Exact figures are unavailable but it seems possible that this engine was giving in excess of 500 bhp. A label on the gearshift consol said 'WARNING VEHICLE MUST OPERATE ON A FUEL HAVING A MINIMUM OF 103 RESEARCH OCTANE AND 95 MOTOR OCTANE OR ENGINE DAMAGE MAY RESULT' and the air cleaner was fitted up inside the hood. Chevrolet fitted an additional gauze filter as a flame arrester, a precaution against blowback when the engine was being revved with the bonnet up. Find an original one of these cars today and your fortune is made.

The normal 427 hood was externally identical to the

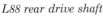

L88 rear drive shaft

L88 and carried striping which related to the interior colour of the car. The engine range included a tri-carb set-up but the hoods on these cars were functional only in as much as they provided clearance for the larger engine.

In mid-1967, production of the Sting Ray stopped and the factory retooled for a new model that was all new in appearance, but its engine, gearbox and power-trains, chassis suspension and steering were identical, ensuring that for owners of '63 to '67 cars, mechanical parts would be plentiful and cheap for years to come. The new car would have all kinds of virtues and some distinct failings, all described in another book in this series. The new car was far better streamlined, the '63 to '67 shape dating back to the 1959 Sting Ray racer and based on the eroneous theory that an upside-down aerofoil section body would give a car downforce. This theory fails principally because it ignores ground effect and various other principles well known to today's designers of even the most humble saloons. Anyone who has driven a '63 to '67 with an unmodified body in excess of 120 mph will have experienced the unpleasant effect of aerodynamic lift at the front of the car when the steering loses its self-centring effect and the car starts to feel light. The power required to force the car through the air at these speeds also makes the rear end tend to squat which compounds the effect.

However, as these cars become more collectable so fewer owners are bothered by this kind of problem.

To drive or restore, the Corvette hobby

The restoration boom came from nowhere in the early seventies to a situation today where the owners of cars covered by this book are all concerned, whether to a greater or lesser extent.

In 1972 GM's own *Corvette News* was able to publish an article about a *concours d'elegance* in Northern California where all the '63 to '67 cars had custom wheels, and their front bumpers removed! Today the correct original wheels even have to mount replicas of the original black, gold or red striped tyres while the bumper support brackets must be the right colour supported with the right size nuts and bolts with the correct head markings.

While it is laudable that these cars should now be returned to their former glory after a useful life at least those 1972 concours cars were driven up to Christian Brothers Vineyards at Nappa Valley under their own power. Today's winning cars inevitably arrive in purpose-built aluminium trailers towed by Chevrolet Suburbans.

A top class restoration can cost in excess of $20,000 even if the majority of the work is done by the owner in his hobby time and at the end he will have a car that is just too expensive to drive on the road.

He is also likely to discover the disappointing truth that a fully restored car will still rattle and squeak more than a modern one, and that the ride and handling will also fall far short of today's standards. Sadly, now that almost all cars have monocoque bodies and all-round

Above right '63–'67s at Bloomington, Indiana, everyones' favourite Corvette meet. Foreground car is a '67 427 coupe

Below right '63 coupes awaiting judging at the Bloomington Show. Later coupes do not have the stainless windscreen surround which extended over the door

independent suspension, our expectations too have improved. He may also discover when he tries to sell his investment that he can only realize half its actual cost because there is a glut of fully restored Corvettes of all ages on the market.

This author quite unashamedly pleads for cars that are daily drivers, kept in good roadworthy condition with components replaced only as and when they deteriorate. If you manage to buy a 1965 fuel-injected convertible, 'running but rough', how much better to take a month off work and enjoy a 2000-mile drive around your particular continent, wining and dining at the best restaurants and hotels every night. Your car will be admired wherever you go by people who couldn't tell the difference between Harrison screws and Corbin spring clamps.

Glove box with original enclosures in 1965. Car comes with air-conditioning

More foolish still is to buy a running car and then have it fully restored by a highly paid specialist. Because of its unique construction, the rustless, solid and easily repaired fibreglass body so readily removed from the massive and almost rust-free chassis, there is nothing very clever about doing a good restoration on a Corvette. You need to check all the books to make sure you are putting all the right parts back correctly and painting them the right colour. Since virtually every part ever used in every Corvette made is available in expensive, reproduction form; if not from Chevrolet, it's really only a matter of putting the bits together.

Restoring a Jaguar, an MGB or a Porsche requires special skills in making imperceptable repairs to rusted-out steelwork. Restoring a Morgan or a pre-war sports car requires the special skill of a joiner. Repairing a

396 Big Block fitted easily into the 1965 engine compartment and spark plug access was actually easier than on the Small Block. Ignition wires had metal braiding to prevent radio interference

Ferrari or an Aston Martin requires ability in dealing with aluminium bodywork and even fabricated panels that are now unobtainable. The Corvette gives you none of these problems, it is just harder to get a good paint finish on a fibreglass car than a metal one. Even the interior presents no great difficulty as seat coverings, door panels and complete carpet sets and dash pads are all available in the correct original colours and materials.

Today's buyer of, say a 1965 coupe might be a young man with few commitments and some spare money who dreamed of owning a Corvette back in 1965 but was only able to build plastic kits and read of his favourite car because he was ten years old at the time. Or an enthusiast in his forties who perhaps had young children then and just lacked space and time to own the car of his dreams.

The collector's ideal is to hear about a car that has been put away in a dry garage since the day it was delivered, or at worst just run in. Hopefully, the car will have been left on blocks to preserve the tyres, have had its coolant drained and light oil poured into the bores and its windows left open just enough to prevent the interior from being too musty.

Ideally the car will have been delivered by the dealer on a trailer and still have the original sticker on the driver's window proclaiming its price and options. Amazingly, such cars really do still turn up, sometimes even with a full list of options and a very early serial number. Discoveries like these are still made because new Corvettes have always been playthings for rich people and not utility vehicles to provide daily service from the day they are bought.

Who knows how many servicemen bought Corvettes before being posted to Vietnam and never returned for them? Such finds are rare but delightful and provide a valuable source of information for restorers and historians.

For every such car there are hundreds which are

Right The author smokes away from the line at Felton drag strip, Northumberland in 1974. 327/350 consistently returned ETs in the low 14s. After eight years of hard use, this car was sold for five times its 1971 purchase price

*Eight air-conditioned
Corvettes awaiting buyers at
a Pompano Beach, Florida
Corvette specialist*

bought through the daily papers or car magazines which, though running, require years of painstaking effort to return them to their former glory. While a typical 1965 Impala will have 200,000 miles, torn seats, a slipping transmission and a very rusty body but be basically stock, the typical Corvette will be rust-free, but will have been modified by well-meaning and fashion-conscious owners perhaps like this.

A new 1965 fuel-injected coupe is delivered to a Pennsylvania dentist, his fourth 'Vette. He fits two extra taillamps, California-style, and a Muntz eight-track tape player under the glove box with stereo speakers cut into the door panels. For 1966 Chevrolet drop fuel injection, so, on a friend's recommendation, the original fuel system is heaved out and a 600CFM Holley on an Edelbrock manifold is substituted and bulge glassed into the hood to accommodate this. He also fits headers and junks the exhaust manifolds. In 1967 he spins the car on the freeway in the wet, has the rear body repaired, the car runs almost straight but the chassis behind wheels is an inch out of true as can be seen by looking at the gas filler beneath the lid. In 1968 the dentist sells the '65 coupe to buy a new '68.

The new owner, who runs a car wash, gives it more California treatment with 7 in. chrome steel wheels and Moon caps, the front bumper is removed complete with all mounting hardware and holes in the fibreglass filled, and the whole car resprayed in metalflake. A new Pioneer eight-track player is fitted between the seats, the armrest cushion discarded and extra speakers cut into the rear compartment panel. The new owner doesn't like the protruding front parking lamps, and has these cut off and filled. By 1970 the headers have rusted through, so a second set is installed complete with chrome side pipes and the rear exhaust outlet holes are blocked in with filler and the bezels discarded. A CB radio is bolted to the top of the dash and a mike clip to the gearshift console, the antenna is on the rear bumper. He sells the car wash to a developer, buys a new LT1 and moves to Florida.

Left Driven to the circuit, this show-standard restored '67 coupe squats its tail under hard acceleration at Goodwood, England

125

Six taillamps, California style, these on a customized 1963

The third owner is a waitress who burns her legs badly on the side pipes so the full system is swapped by the parking-lot kid and grafted on to his '64. He gives her his old manifolds and an abbreviated system which terminates in turbo mufflers just ahead of the rear axle. The side trims now show holes and slots where the side pipes were, but her legs heal perfectly.

In 1972 the waitress follows a New York customer to his Village apartment for the weekend. Uplifting for her, but thieves break the ventipane pivots, and steal the Delco radio and the eight-track. Six months later she marries the New Yorker who buys her a 454 convertible and sells the coupe to a *Hot Rod* reading engineering graduate, who gives it a Mako nose from Motion at Baldwin, 8 in. Cragars at front and 10 in. at rear all

running 60-profile Micky Thompson cross-plys. Motion make a beautiful job flaring all the wheel openings.

Said *Hot Rod* reader fits an Accel twin point distributor with no tach drive, a Hurst gearshift, Kenwood stereo radio cassette sideways in the old radio aperture and removes the spare wheel carrier to save weight.

*Hot Rod*der marries in 1973 and drives his bride all the way to Mexico for the honeymoon. The brakes feel increasingly awful but they can't be fixed in Mexico so they settle for a full-buttoned velvet interior for 125 greenbacks. The brakes dissapear at the border, running over the US customs inspector's foot. In San Diego the Chevy dealer recommends that the bores are so rusty that only $1000 worth of new calipers will solve the

1963 fuel injection, first year of new style plenum chamber. All '63–'65s with fuel injection had cold air induction

problem. The *Hot Rod* reader trades his 'Vette and $1000 for a Camaro Z28 with a 'real' back axle and air-conditioning.

The Chevy dealer stores the car for three years until 1977 when he advertises it in *Hemmings* as an 'Original Southern California car with low mileage, runs good, needs restoration'. The car is bought by a mature Pennsylvania engineer who flies to San Diego with four stainless steel sleeved calipers from Tech Automotive, which he fits before driving the car home, east.

Averaging 75 mph for the journey he gets ten speeding tickets in seven states but when you've got a '65 fuel-injected coupe, who cares? What he does care about is that after five days of struggling to free just eight body mounting bolts, he finally lifts the body off the chassis to find that the original build order still glued to the gas tank says his car was delivered from St. Louis to his local Chevy dealer right there in Pennsylvania.

Six years later in 1983, after thousands of hours of intermittant hard work, hundreds of telephone calls and 11,000 dollars spent on parts, he meets a dentist at his local Corvette club whose eighth Corvette is the first '84 in town. The dentist tells him he used to have a 'Vette just like his, and bought it new.

Trailered!

American model years and VINs

Whilst in Europe we accept the date of first registration as the manufacture date, American cars are identified by model year. American manufacturers traditionally introduce face-lifted models each autumn and any American car has specific characteristics relating only to that year. A number or letter in the Vehicle Identification Number (the VIN) identifies the year and since 1968, its number has been visible on the left-hand windscreen pillar, seen through the glass.

For the Corvettes covered by this book the locations of the stamped VIN tags are as follows. From 1953 until early 1960 the plate is on the driver's door post. On the rest of the live-axled production, the plate is on the bottom part of the steering column under the hood. On 1963–67 cars it is riveted to a horizontal reinforcing member which runs underneath the glovebox.

The model year is three months out of phase with the calendar year. For example the 1965 Corvette, the last with itallic Sting Ray badges and stainless rear exhaust pipe bezels, and the first with disc brakes and functional louvres behind the front wheels, might have been manufactured any time from the beginning of September 1964 when the assembly plant re-opened after retooling, to the mid-summer of 1965 when it would have closed for the annual holiday of assembly line workers and the small amount of retooling necessary for the very similar 1966 model. Since demand is usually at its highest with the announcement of face-lifted models at the beginning of the new model year, approximately one third of the 1965 models will have actually been made during the calendar year of 1964. The VIN numbers vary as follows:

Year	VIN no.	Total production		Base price	
		Conv.	Coupé	Conv.	Coupé
1953	E53F001001–E53F001300	300		$3498	
1954	E54S001001–E54S004640	3640		$2774	
*1955	VE555001001–VE55S001700	700		$2909	
1956	E56S001001–E56S004467	3467		$2900	
1957	E57S100001–E57S106339	6339		$3176	
1958	J58S100001–J58S109168	9168		$3591	
1959	J59S100001–J59S109670	9670		$3875	
1960	00867S100001–00867S110261	10,261		$3872	
1961	10867S100001–10867S110939	10,939		$3934	
1962	20867S100001–20867S114531	14,531		$4038	
**1963	30867S100001–30867S121513	10,919	10,594	$4037	$4257
1964	40867S100001–40867S122229	13,925	8304	$4037	$4252
1965	194675S100001–194675S123562	15,376	8186	$4106	$4321
1966	194676S100001–194676S127720	17,762	9958	$4084	$4295
1967	194677S100001–194677S122940	14,436	8504	$4240	$4388

*Note: six-cylinder cars did not have the V prefix

**Note: for '63 to '67 coupes fourth and fifth digits are 37. In GM parlance, a '37' is a coupe, a '67' a convertible and this system continued until 1977.

Specifications

Basic dimensions	'53 to '55	'56 to '57	'58 to '62	'63 to '67
Overall length	13 ft 11 in.	14 ft 0 in.	14 ft $9\frac{1}{2}$ in.	14 ft $7\frac{1}{2}$ in.
Overall width	6 ft 0 in.	5 ft $10\frac{1}{2}$ in.	6 ft $0\frac{1}{2}$ in.	5 ft 9 in.
Overall height	4 ft 4 in.	4 ft 4 in.	4 ft $4\frac{1}{2}$ in.	3 ft $11\frac{3}{4}$ in.
Front track	4 ft 9 in.	4 ft 9 in.	4 ft 9 in.	4 ft $8\frac{3}{4}$ in.
Rear track	4 ft 11 in.	4 ft 11 in.	4 ft 11 in.	4 ft $9\frac{1}{2}$ in.
Wheelbase	8 ft 6 in.	8 ft 6 in.	8 ft 6 in.	8 ft 2 in.
Kerb weight	2850 lb	2880 lb	3080 lb	3130 lb
Front/rear weight distribution (%)	53/47	52/48	53/47	48/52

RPO no.	Capacity (cu. in.)	Bore/stroke (in.)	cr:1	Max. bhp @ rpm	Carburettor	Year available
Straight sixes						
—	235	$3\frac{9}{16} \times 3\frac{15}{56}$	8.0	150 @ 4200	3 × Carter	'53, '54
—	235	$3\frac{9}{16} \times 3\frac{15}{16}$	8.0	155 @ 4200	3 × Carter	'55
V8 Small Blocks						
—	265	$3\frac{3}{4} \times 3$	8.0	195 @ 5000	1 × 4-Carter	'55
—	265	$3\frac{3}{4} \times 3$	9.25	210 @ 5200	1 × 4-Carter	'56
469	265	$3\frac{3}{4} \times 3$	9.25	225 @ 5200	2 × 4-Carter	'56
448	265	$3\frac{3}{4} \times 3$	9.25	240 @ 5200	1 × 4-Carter	'56
449	265	$3\frac{3}{4} \times 3$	9.25	240 @ 5200	2 × 4-Carter	'56
—	283	$3\frac{7}{8} \times 3$	9.5	229 @ 4800	1 × 4-Carter	'57
469A	283	$3\frac{7}{8} \times 3$	9.5	245 @ 5000	2 × 4-Carter	'57
469B	283	$3\frac{7}{8} \times 3$	9.5	270 @ 6000	2 × 4-Carter	'57
579A	283	$3\frac{7}{8} \times 3$	9.5	250 @ 5000	F/injection	'57
579B	283	$3\frac{7}{8} \times 3$	10.5	283 @ 6200	F/injection	'57
—	283	$3\frac{7}{8} \times 3$	9.5	230 @ 4800	1 × 4-Carter	'58, '59, '60, '61
469	283	$3\frac{7}{8} \times 3$	9.5	245 @ 5000	2 × 4-Carter	'58, '59, '60, '61

469C	283	$3\frac{7}{8} \times 3$	9.5	270 @ 6000	2 × 4-Carter	'58, '59, '60
579	283	$3\frac{7}{8} \times 3$	9.5	250 @ 5000	F/injection	'58, '59
579D	283	$3\frac{7}{8} \times 3$	9.5	290 @ 6200	F/injection	'58, '59
579	283	$3\frac{7}{8} \times 3$	11.0	275 @ 5200	F/injection	'60
579D	283	$3\frac{7}{8} \times 3$	11.0	315 @ 6200	F/injection	'60
468	283	$3\frac{7}{8} \times 3$	9.5	270 @ 6000	2 × 4-Carter	'61
353	283	$3\frac{7}{8} \times 3$	11.0	275 @ 5200	F/injection	'61
354	283	$3\frac{7}{8} \times 3$	11.0	315 @ 6200	F/injection	'61
—	327	$4 \times 3\frac{1}{4}$	10.5	250 @ 4400	1 × 4-Carter	'62, '63, '64, '65
583	327	$4 \times 3\frac{1}{4}$	10.5	300 @ 5000	1 × 4-Carter	'62
396	327	$4 \times 3\frac{1}{4}$	11.25	340 @ 6000	1 × 4-Carter	'62
582	327	$4 \times 3\frac{1}{4}$	11.25	360 @ 6000	F/injection	'62
L75	327	$4 \times 3\frac{1}{4}$	10.5	300 @ 5000	1 × 4-Carter	'63, '64, '65
L76	327	$4 \times 3\frac{1}{4}$	11.25	340 @ 6000	1 × 4-Carter	'63
L84	327	$4 \times 3\frac{1}{4}$	11.25	360 @ 6000	F/injection	'63
L76	327	$4 \times 3\frac{1}{4}$	11.25	365 @ 6200	1 × 4-Holley	'64, '65
L84	327	$4 \times 3\frac{1}{4}$	11.25	375 @ 6200	F/injection	'64, '65
L79	327	$4 \times 3\frac{1}{4}$	11.0	350 @ 5800	1 × 4-Holley	'65, '66, '67
L79	327	$4 \times 3\frac{1}{4}$	10.5	300 @ 5000	1 × 4-Holley	'66, '67

V8 Big Blocks

L78	396	$4\frac{3}{32} \times 3\frac{49}{64}$	11.0	425 @ 6400	1 × 4-Holley	'65
L36	427	$4\frac{1}{4} \times 3\frac{49}{64}$	10.25	390 @ 5400	1 × 4-Holley	'66, '67
L72	427	$4\frac{1}{4} \times 3\frac{49}{66}$	11.00	425 @ 6400	1 × 4-Holley	'66
L68	427	$4\frac{1}{4} \times 3\frac{49}{64}$	10.25	400 @ 5400	3 × 2-Holley	'67
L71	427	$4\frac{1}{4} \times 3\frac{49}{64}$	11.00	435 @ 5800	3 × 2-Holley	'67
L88	427	$4\frac{1}{4} \times 3\frac{49}{64}$	12.5	430*	1 × 4-Holley	'67

*believed to exceed 500, see text

Bibliography

There are more than 50 Corvette books on the market, and the author adds this, his second on the subject, to the pile. Some of the recent picture books are misleadingly inaccurate but those listed below are works of impeccable scholarship and should be in any Corvette owner's library.

Corvette; America's Star Spangled Sports Car by Karl Ludvigsen, Automobile Quarterly Publications, 2nd edition, 1978

The Complete Corvette Restoration and Technical Guide—Volume 1 by Noland Adams, Automobile Quarterly Publications, 1980

The Corvette Black Book 1953–1984 Super De Luxe edition, Michael Bruce Associates Inc., 1983

The Illustrated Corvette Buyers Guide by Michael Antonick, Motorbooks International, 1983

Harley Earl and the Dream Machine by Stephen Bailey, Weidenfeld & Nicolson, London, 1983

Vette Vues Fact Book 1963–67 Sting Ray by N. F. Dobbins, 6th edition, Glenside, PA, 1984

Road & Track on Corvette 1953–67, Brooklands Books, London

Cars of the 50s and 60s by Michael Sedgwick, Temple Press, London, 1983

The Best of Corvette News edited by Karl Ludvigsen, Automobile Quarterly Publications, 1976

Acknowledgements

The author would particularly like to thank all those who have helped in the preparation of this book. Special thanks to Bill Mitchell and Zora Arkus Duntov for agreeing to be interviewed, and to Bill Locke, Associate Editor of *Vette Vues* magazine. Also to the Kirks family of Washington D.C., Ken Jestes, Lowri Potts and the British Film Institute Archive Library.

Most of the pictures of the early cars were supplied by Bill Locke of *Vette Vues* magazine. Further photographs were supplied by *Corvette News*, GM Photographic, Chevrolet Public Relations, GM Design, Ed Alexander, Chuck Harransky, Graham Oliver, Terry Sims and Robin Summers. All other photographs by the author. Drawings by David Hoy.

Index

A
air-conditioning   **79, 93, 96**
Antwerp   **53**
Aston Martin   **91, 120**

B
Barstow, Arizona   **9, 13**
Birmingham   **106**
Bloomington Show,
  Indiana   **116–117**
Borg-Warner   **43, 96**
brakes   **33, 97–99, 102, 106–107,
  127**
Buick 'Y-job'   **14**

C
CBS   **12**
Cadillac   **26, 46, 55**
California   **125–126, 128**
Campbell-Ewald Advertising
  Agency   **37**
Cessna   **35**
Chevrolet
  150   **14, 42**
  210   **14**
  LT1   **125**
  Bel Air   **11, 14**
  Camaro Z28   **113, 128**
  Corvette
    '53   **9, 16–17, 20, 23, 28–30,
      32, 35, 44, 46, 55, 80, 129–130**
    '54   **19–25, 30, 32, 44, 46, 80,
      129–130**
    '55   **9, 26–27, 30–32, 44,
      46–47, 80, 129–130**
    '56   **19, 30–47, 80, 129–130**
    '57   **31–47, 52–53, 80, 129–130**

    '58   **32, 46–80, 129–130**
    '59   **32, 46–80, 115, 129–130**
    '60   **32, 46–80, 129–130**
    '61   **32, 46–80, 129–130**
    '62   **32, 46–80, 129–130**
    '63   **46, 55, 80–97, 99, 112,
      115–117, 126–127, 129–130**
    '64   **46, 80–97, 115–117, 126,
      129–130**
    '65   **46, 94, 97–120, 125–130**
    '66   **46, 94, 97–117, 125,
      129–130**
    '67   **46, 94, 97–117, 125,
      129–130**
    '68   **125**
    '82   **46**
    '84   **46, 128**
    '85   **11**
    EX122   **15**
    Sting Ray   **55, 59, 63, 80–97,
      99, 104, 115, 129**
  Pontiac   **102–104**
Chevrolet Suburban   **116**
Chicago   **9**
Christian Brothers
  Vineyards   **116**
Chrysler   **14, 47**
Cole, Ed   **16, 37**
Columbia Pictures   **10**
Corbett, Glenn   **9**
Corvette News   **116**
Cunningham, Briggs   **55**

D
Daytona Beach, Florida   **37**
Detroit   **64**
Duntov, Zora Arkus   **37**

E
Earl, Harley   **14**
Eisenhower, Dwight   **9**

F
Felton, Northumberland   **120**
Ferrari   **55, 92, 104, 113, 120**
Fitch, John   **37, 55**
Flint, Michigan   **14, 20**
Florida   **87, 125**
Ford Motor Company   **14, 37, 47**
France   **15, 106**

G
General Motors   **14–16, 42, 49,
  53, 55, 80, 85, 91, 94, 107, 113,
  116, 130**
Goodwood   **125**
Grossman, Bob   **55**

H
Halibrand   **55**
handling   **43, 46, 56**
Hansgen, Walt   **37**
hardtop   **45, 49, 51**
Hawaii   **78**
Hemmings   **128**
Hiller, Arthur   **12**
Holley   **96, 110, 125**
Horton, Johnny   **13**
Hot Rod   **126–128**

I
Inverness, Scotland   **53**

134

INDEX

J
Jaguar **26, 32, 55, 92, 119**
Jordan, Chuck **55**

K
Kleber tyres **15**

L
L88 **112–115**
Lancashire, England **53**
Le Mans 24 hours **55**
Le Sabre **14**
Long Beach **13**
Los Angeles **9**
Lotus **92**

M
MGB **119**
Maharis, George **9–12**
Maranello **113**
Marlboro MD Raceway **80**
Maserati **92**
Mercedes-Benz **43**
Mexico **127**
Milner, Martin **9–12**

Missouri **9**
Morgan **119**
Motion, Baldwin **126**
Motorama Show **9, 14–15, 29, 26, 31–32, 35**
Muncie gearbox **96, 107**

N
Nappa Valley **116**
New York **14, 126**

P
Paris Show **15**
Pennsylvania **125, 128**
Pikes Peak hillclimb **42**
Pompano Beach, Florida **123**
Porsche **46, 55, 92, 119**
Powerglide **20, 45–46**

R
Riddle, Nelson **13**
Road & Track **37**
Rochester fuel injection **11, 42–43, 96, 99, 127**
Route 66 **8–13**

S
St Louis **9, 17, 20, 128**
San Diego **127–128**
Sebring **37**
sidescreens **38**
Silliphant, Sterling **12**

T
Tech Automotive **128**
tyres **43, 52, 85, 100**

V
VIN **129–130**

W
Waldorf Hotel **14**
wheels **52, 80, 93, 100, 106, 113**
Williams, Hank **13**
Wonder Bar **13**

X
XP300 **14**